The Little Book of Passage

Libretto di transito

Franca Mancinelli

Translated from the Italian by John Taylor

BITTER OLEANDER
P R E S S

The Bitter Oleander Press
4983 Tall Oaks Drive
Fayetteville, New York 13066-9776
USA

www.bitteroleander.com
info@bitteroleander.com

Original title: *Libretto di transito*, Amos Edizioni, 2018

Copyright © 2018 Preface & English translation by John Taylor

Copyright © 2018 Amos Edizioni for the original Italian poems. Amos
Edizioni, www.amosedizioni.it, series: A27 poesia, No. 4

Franca Mancinelli holds the rights for the translation of any or all of these
Italian poems into all other languages

ISBN #: 978-0-9993279-2-0

Library of Congress Control Number: 2018949069

Cover Design & Layout: Roderick Martinez

Cover artwork: photograph, from the series "Segni" ("Signs"), 2005-2009,
by Sabrina Mezzaqui. Copyright © Sabrina Mezzaqui

Photograph of Franca Mancinelli by Enrico Chiaretti

Manufactured in the United States of America

The author and the translator would like to thank Paul B. Roth for publishing nine of these poems in the Spring 2018 issue of *The Bitter Oleander*, Daniel Lawless for publishing seven of these poems in the April 2018 issue of *Plume*, and Denis Boyle for publishing eleven poems, in March, in *The Fortnightly Review*. An excerpt from the introduction appeared, as a review of the original Italian book, in the *Times Literary Supplement*. The entire introduction was translated into Italian (by Riccardo Frolloni) and published on the website of the Research Center PENS (Poesia Contemporanea e Nuove Scritture), at the University of Salento in May, 2018.

TABLE OF CONTENTS

CONTENTS

Filling the Gaps: Franca Mancinelli's *Little Book of Passage*

Franca Mancinelli's *Libretto di transito* appeared in 2018, after her first two books of poetry, *Mala kruna* (2007) and *Pasta madre* (2013), won several prizes and established her as a compelling new voice in contemporary Italian writing. In *Mala kruna,* she explores an individual's relationship to the Other and to otherness (the title means "little crown" in Serbo-Croatian), often in the context of love and the quest for selfhood; and then, in *Pasta madre* (literally "mother dough"), she focuses on the "original dough" with its "living yeast" of nature and poetic language, that is, the primordial elements to which she must time and again appeal to seek out genuine wholesome resources. Vivid, unusual, often intense imagery emphasizes her remove from this vital nourishment as well as its curative potential whenever she encounters it. The poems evoke privileged moments, often taking place between sleeping and waking, when brief communions with this primal, hope-fostering "dough" become possible, or, on the contrary, when she senses her separation from it even more acutely.

Composed of thirty-three prose poems and brief narratives, this new book turns to short poetic prose after the equally short and subtle verse poetry of her two earlier books. What does this formal change imply? A slight increase in storytelling, though in the most fragmentary sense of the term. Mancinelli might well designate a setting (a train car), suggest that she is traveling alone ("without knowing what brings me to you"), mention a gaze which she directs out the window and which, by means of a reflection on the pane, offers an imaginary glimpse, even a prolonged view of that missing "you" who now seems superposed on the pane as well as on the landscape rushing by (almost as if he were actually sitting across from her), but the haunting quality of such texts lies less in their succinct "plots" *per se* than in what is suggested by them: in this case, the unstated emotion that makes the other's absence so present and enables the narrator to "read," as the same piece concludes, "into your face until light came." Not to mention the feelings that evolve from this rich mental and emotional experience and surely remain alive beyond, as it were, the time and setting of the text. Other events perhaps subsequently take place—or not. This we do not know. "The story continues in silence," as the poet phrases it elsewhere.

As in her verse poetry, which similarly points to silence as it sketches moods, daydreams, and fantasies set amid carefully observed daily scenes, Mancinelli's short prose revolves around unvoiced centers and disturbing causes which cannot be wholly defined yet which have come to the surface, as it were. As the reader meditates on them, they reveal their intricacy and mystery. That is, wordless centers full of emotions, thoughts, perceptions, and even imaginable acts—those pertaining, for instance, to the loss or lack of something or someone essential. Or perhaps I should say, more cautiously, that the contents of these centers, the "hearts of the matter" (as I am tempted to call them), cannot yet, or readily, be designated and named. This is why the epigraph—"To fill a Gap / Insert the Thing that caused it"—by Emily Dickinson is so apt. Many of these prose poems derive from or indicate gaps: the distance between two places or two human beings; a breach in a continuity that must be healed or sealed, perhaps by the "clay" that another human being applies to the "broken, empty places"; an abyss, modest or more dramatic, that suddenly gapes open, like that "widening crack" associated with a train rushing by and that announces "something enormous for which we still have to wait." Like Dickinson's "Thing," this "something" is substantial yet not completely clear-cut: we sense it deeply, it definitely exists, yet it is not entirely definite. But we must try to fill the gap as best we can.

In all events, an unsettling emotion, a "motion" that we sense in our minds and bodies in certain circumstances, especially when we are faced with what Mancinelli calls a "faglia"—a "fault" (as in geology), a "fault line," a "flaw," or a "rift" that must be repaired, healed, sealed. Water is an equally important, usually positive recurrent element. "In the morning something inside your body was moving," she writes in one text, "a water crossed by its current." Significantly, movement is depicted often here, including several other train trips, with suitcases to pack or unpack, and "things you have forgotten to take with you." Some prose poems, moreover, hint at potentially life-changing (inner or outer) movements that are taking place, have taken place, or might take place in the near future. In one text, which opens with a stationary image, a nearly full "glass of water on the table," the poet moves from looking at that water to recalling the shifting colors of the seawater where she and other children used to play; but as she recollects, the colors form a net and a "dark lure" becomes visible in the watery depths. Now an adult, she is remembering the end of childhood (a salient theme here):

A glass of water on the table, by chance almost full after dinner. We were alone and transparent, with something burning inside. One color after another, and then different colors, together, as in a bright moving net. The blue rose from the ankles all the way up to where we could still talk. Then something touched us. Its dark lure was submerged in the water.

And even as the passage from childhood to adulthood often implies essential and sometimes painful separations—those "gaps," "breaches" and "fault lines," once again—one notices often, in Mancinelli's writing, an effort to confront other kinds of disunities as well: mankind and nature, the inner world of sensibility and the outer world of brute facts. The interplay between "I" and "you" is particularly intriguing as the poet sometimes employs "you" to designate herself. Above all, she movingly uses autobiographical details to raise more general psychological and philosophical issues. Elsewhere, the delicate, fragmentary, narrative architectures that she so deftly builds rely less on elements from the real world than on metaphors or even dreamlike imagery. In one prose poem, the narrator "was a house inhabited by plants sticking out into the empty air"; in another text, an initial realistic image— bending over a mud puddle—evolves into an oneiric scene involving an archetypal "ritual," a rite of passage:

You bend over a mud puddle. Cover your face with your hands and make it dark. The eye sockets remain. From your fingertips to your shoulders, the earth caresses you. The bright white teeth call out to the submerged bones. A big sea animal sleeps beneath the sand. The ritual is almost concluded.

The book concludes with a beneficial metaphorical tree whose leaves are "thinking up a sentence for you." In fact, all the pieces in this book, taken one after another, seemingly sketch out a single overarching story—a movement towards healing or renewal.

This brings me to the second epigraph, by Simone Weil. "L'arbre est en vérité enraciné dans le ciel" can be paraphrased as "To tell the truth, trees are rooted in the sky." Of course, Weil's "en vérité," which is sometimes translated as "verily," can also be rendered by "in fact" or "actually"; but I would like to emphasize the seriousness with which Mancinelli seeks kinds of truth through her sober, circumspect practice of writing, which eschews all rhetorical flourishes that might blur her focus and scrutiny. As in Weil's maxim, the real world in its multifarious forms possesses, for Mancinelli, a less immediately accessible or perceptible origin than the mere ground on which we walk (though note her contrasting images, here and there, about shoes or feet pressing down or weighing down on the earth, all reminders not only to peer into existence as profoundly as possible, but also not to lose touch with it in the process). Similarly, maybe the roots of a life take their nourishment (or their poison) from secret "fault lines"; maybe they also culminate in some kind of "sky" or "heaven" (the French "ciel" means both). There is always more to what one sees or senses; in all events, the genuine sources of what we feel, think, dream, and do remain at a remove, and it is the task of poetry to try to bridge those gaps or at least to show where the bridges might be built. Arguably, Weil's "sky" or "heaven" should be equated, for these poetic prose texts, less with a transcendental horizon than with sensibility in the fullest sense, encompassing the unconscious, memories, dreams, daydreams, and a very heightened awareness— the intricate mixture of thinking and feeling in a human being facing that tree, that other person, or herself.

Mancinelli writes clear, concise, artfully allusive Italian. The ambiguities and enigmas that fascinate in her work stem from the type of events and feelings that she explores, not from any stylistic haziness. With the poet's generous and meticulous help, I have nearly everywhere been able to keep the English close to the Italian. Yet let me add a word about the title. Literally "Libretto of Transit," the polysemous Italian title called, from the onset, for a less immediately literal interpretation. First of all, our English word "libretto" is associated with opera, whereas the Italian word possesses this meaning but also others that are active in everyday parlance. For example, a "libretto" can also be a booklet, a pamphlet, or even a small manual such as a "libretto d'istruzioni" ("instruction manual or booklet"). Secondly, the musical sense of "libretto" is not put forward by Mancinelli, but rather that of a relatively short book—very thoughtfully put together, by the way, through key words, images, emotions, or scenes that provide transitions from one text to the next. Similarly, although "transito" means "transit," and "passeggeri in transito" means "passengers in transit," semantic differences between the two cognates occur in such an expression as "uccelli di transito" ("birds of passage") and when "transito" signifies "passing away," "death." In the texts themselves, death is conjured up a few times, whence the motivation to seek out an English word that would be, in addition, less technical and juridical in tone than "transit" and could also bring out some of these other Italian meanings. Needless to say, the subject matter and the very writing of this book trace out a transition, a passage. Almost like a notebook, these captivating texts have accompanied the poet on her way. Hence, *The Little Book of Passage*.

John Taylor
Saint-Barthélemy d'Anjou
April 16, 2018

The Little Book of Passage

Libretto di transito

To fill a Gap
Insert the Thing that caused it—

Emily Dickinson

L'arbre est en vérité enraciné dans le ciel

Simone Weil

Non è solo preparare una valigia. È confezionarsi, vestirsi bene.
Entrare nella taglia esatta della pena. Gesti a una destinazione
sola. Calzando scarpe che non hanno mai premuto la terra,
dormiremo nel centro dello sguardo, come neonati.

It's not just packing a suitcase. It's primping and preening oneself. Entering into the exact size of the punishment. All acts aimed at a single destination. Wearing shoes that have never pressed down on the earth, we will sleep at the center of the gaze, like newborn children.

A volte un breve annuncio ricorda la linea gialla, a volte è soltanto un rumore che si avvicina. La fenditura che si apre dev'essere arginata subito con le mani che si aggrappano a qualcosa, gli occhi chiusi. Ci si stringe alla panca, agli oggetti che si hanno con sé, fino a che il treno trascorre al nostro fianco. Con il tremore di qualcosa di enorme, per cui dobbiamo ancora aspettare.

Sometimes a brief warning recalls the yellow line, sometimes it's just a noise approaching. Suddenly hands must stop up the widening crack by gripping at something, eyes shut. We cling to the benches, to objects brought along, until the train rushes by. Shaking like something enormous for which we still have to wait.

Viaggio senza sapere cosa mi porta a te. So che stai andando oltre i confini del foglio, dei campi coltivati. È il tuo modo di venirmi incontro: come un'acqua in cammino, diramando. Guardando dal finestrino, ti ho letto nel viso finché c'era luce.

Traveling without knowing what brings me to you. I know you're going beyond the limits of the sheet of paper, of the cultivated fields. It's your way of coming face to face with me: like water in its course, branching off. Looking out the window, I kept reading into your face until light came.

Le cose che hai scordato di portare con te. Lasciate negli scompartimenti dei treni, scivolate dai sedili degli autobus. A un tratto ti raggiungono premendo l'angolo duro della loro assenza, come attraversando una zona più limpida dello sguardo.

Things you have forgotten to take with you. Left inside
train compartments, slipped off bus seats. All of a sudden
they catch up with you, pressing the acute point of their
absence, while crossing a clearer zone of your gaze.

La sera, con una sigaretta tra le dita, guardando il cielo scurirsi come terra bagnata, mio padre annaffia. Quando è laggiù, nascosto dalle piante dei pomodori, nell'angolo più lontano del giardino, posso sentire dal pozzo l'acqua versarsi e scendere tra i granuli, fino alle radici dove è attesa. Qui, dove il flusso si perde, crescono erbe dure dal piccolo fiore, piante dal frutto velenoso. Ma non riesco a zapparle via, non riesco a riparare la falda.

In the evening, a cigarette between his fingers, watching the sky darken like moistened soil, my father waters his garden. When he's standing down there in the farthest corner, hidden by the tomato plants, I can hear the water pouring from the well, streaming down between the dirt clods to the roots awaiting it. Here, where the flow has trickled out, sprout plants with poisonous fruit, stiff stalks of grass with tiny flowers. I haven't succeeded in hoeing them away, in repairing the water table.

Ero una casa abitata da piante che si sporgono ai vuoti, sottili si avvolgono dentro il franare dei muri. Si è dimenticata la porta, questa casa, l'ha inghiottita come un boccone messo un po' di traverso. È così che vengono e vanno: rondini in cerca di rifugio e poi libere gridano di piacere.

I was a house inhabited by plants sticking out into the empty air, skinny ones enveloping themselves inside the cracked walls. A house that had forgotten its door, having swallowed it like a morsel stuck sideways in the throat. And so the swallows come and go, seeking shelter, then free to squeal in pleasure.

Nessuno calma il grido. Non c'è niente da donare in pasto. Non si dorme con questi che chiedono cibo, grattano con il becco e le unghie, in volo spezzato, sporco su ogni cosa. La mattina le strade, e il loro grido insaziato. La grande ciotola della piazza.

No one soothes the squealing. There's nothing to be tossed out as a treat. One can't sleep alongside those who beg for food, scratch with beak and nail, in their broken flight, dirtying everything. In the morning the streets and their insatiable squealing. The big bowl of the square.

Un bicchiere d'acqua sul tavolo, quasi colmo per caso dopo la cena. Eravamo limpidi e soli, con qualcosa che bruciava dentro. Un colore prima di un altro, e poi diversi, insieme, come in una rete che si muove luminosa. L'azzurro saliva dalle caviglie, fino a dove potevamo ancora parlare. Poi ci ha toccati. Si è immerso nell'acqua il suo oscuro richiamo.

A glass of water on the table, by chance almost full after dinner. We were alone and transparent, with something burning inside. One color after another, and then different colors, together, as in a bright moving net. The blue rose from the ankles all the way up to where we could still talk. Then something touched us. Its dark lure was submerged in the water.

L'acqua del fiume è nera. Non ti ci puoi specchiare. Vedi, è accaduto così. Ci siamo trovati nel mirino: piccoli passi nello stesso piccolo cerchio. L'intera città fluttuava. Se ci avesse sfiorato porteremmo segni sul corpo, sottili e rossi lineamenti come dopo il passaggio di una medusa.

Appostato sull'orlo di un tetto il cecchino aspettava. Sapeva ci saremmo incontrati in quel punto, dove si incrocia lo spazio nel tempo, dove si apre la sua pupilla. Quando ha visto passarci di mano lo stesso bicchiere, ci ha sfilati dagli altri. Barcollanti, ci ha guidati a ritrovare l'equilibrio, seguendo il fiume nero, così nero che avremmo potuto calpestarlo. Ogni cosa faceva restando invisibile, governandoci nel cerchio del mirino. Cercava per noi una parete, nascosta da cespugli, grigia, dove finirci lasciandoci calzare le scarpe. Accovacciati o goffamente retti sui piedi, in una intercapedine della notte. Quante volte premuti contro l'intonaco, sbattuti contro il pietrisco, per vedere cosa filtrava da noi.

Una scossa ti ha attraversato senza creparti la fronte. L'hai detto in una lingua soltanto tua.

The river water is black. You can't mirror yourself in it. You see, this is how it happened. We found ourselves targeted: small footsteps in the same small circle. The whole city was floating. If it had brushed up against us, we would bear signs on our bodies, thin red lineaments as when a jellyfish grazes you.

Lurking on the edge of a roof, the sniper was waiting. He knew we would meet at this point, where space crosses time, where the pupil of his eye opens. When he saw us passing the same glass back and forth between us, he took us away from the others. As we were staggering, he guided us so we'd recover our balance, following the black river, so black we could have walked on it. Since everything he did remained invisible, he directed us into his sights. He was seeking a wall for us, hidden by bushes, gray, where he could finish us off, letting us keep our shoes on. Crouching or clumsily standing straight, in a cavity of the night. How many times were we pressed against the plaster, beaten against the rubble, to see what would leak out from us.

A shock has run you through without splitting your forehead. You've said it in a language all your own.

Ecco il fiume che mi allarga lo sguardo, che mi attraversa la fronte. Lo aspetto ogni volta. So quando arriva dal diverso rumore che fanno le rotaie sul ponte. Accanto al sedile una piccola valigia. L'ho preparata sapendo di andare. Sospendendo un attimo i gesti che piegavano e riponevano, ho deglutito allontanando il sapore. Così fanno gli adulti, nascondono per proseguire.

Here's the river which widens my gaze, which flows through my forehead. Each time I await it. I know when it's coming because the rails make a different noise on the bridge. Next to my seat is a small suitcase. I packed it, knowing I was leaving. Breaking off for a moment the movements that were bending down and placing, I swallowed yet kept the taste at a distance. Adults do this, hiding to keep going.

È sempre qui che ci incontriamo, in questo campo di forze dove puoi trovarti sulla bocca il silenzio di un altro. Nessuna presenza, nessuna costanza delle cose. La voce e i gesti governati dalla frequenza di una stazione non raggiunta.

It's always here where we meet, in this force field where you can find another's silence on your lips. No presence, no constancy of things. Voice and movements ruled by the unfound frequency of a radio station.

È accaduto qualcosa tra le ombre. Come cadendo, precipitando a capofitto. Lo so che tu parli e apri la bocca, come un bambino che scoppia in pianto mentre è costretto a mangiare. In quella poltiglia che ti chiude la gola, c'è tutto quanto ti portavo sulla tavola: i doni di un Natale incredibile che continuava con le sue lucine intermittenti. Mi piaceva mettere la barba bianca che picca e stringe con un elastico le tempie. Vedere come lentamente ti affidi. Sorridi e porti alla bocca, ti nutri. Io con il costume rosso e le braccia aperte a versare anche quello che non avevi scritto nella letterina. Ora mi sono tolto la barba. Non mi riconosci? Non ho nessuna parola da dirti. Non ne voglio parlare.

Something happened amid the shadows. Like falling, rushing headlong. I know that you speak and open your mouth, like a child bursting into tears when he is forced to eat. In that mash stuck in your throat is everything I brought to your table: the gifts of an incredible Christmas that kept on going with its blinking lights. I liked putting on a white beard that stung when I tightened it around my temples with a rubber band. To see how slowly you would trust me. You were smiling and bringing food to your mouth, feeding yourself. I in my red costume and with my open arms to deliver as well what you hadn't written down in your little letter. Now I've taken off my beard. Don't you recognize me? I have nothing to say to you. I don't want to talk about it.

Con quanta fermezza resta in piedi su pochi centimetri di tacchi. Con quanto coraggio si è dipinta il viso in un segnale. Eppure è una sola la parte, sempre la stessa: deve credere in lui completamente. Amare i suoi gesti calibrati, i suoi occhi in un punto lontano. Legarsi caviglie e polsi alla sua mancanza. Non tremare, non sciogliersi per troppo desiderio. Rimanere così, dentro una sagoma; incompiuta, perfetta per un lancio di coltelli.

How firmly she stands on a few inches of heels. How bravely she has painted her face into a signal. Yet this is only one part, always the same: she must completely believe in him. Love his calibrated movements, his eyes staring at a distant point. Binding ankles and wrists to his absence. Not trembling, not melting, through too much desire. Remaining like this, inside a silhouette; unfinished, perfect for a knife throw.

Si aggirano tra le stanze di una casa dove sembra arriverà qualcuno, dov'è l'ombra di qualcuno che se n'è andato da poco. Se li fermi e chiedi loro *che cosa,* rispondono *niente.* Si placano soltanto lungo le rive. Poi il modo per dire di essere ancora lì, è raccogliere un sasso e lanciarlo. Ma la pura infanzia dell'acqua ne è scossa, e infranta fino al suo letto di sabbia.

They're wandering among the rooms of a house where it seems that someone will show up, where the shadow of someone who has just left is still lingering. If you stop and ask them *what*, they answer *nothing*. They calm down only along the shores. Then their way of saying they're still there is to pick up a pebble and throw it. But the pure childhood of the water is shaken by this, shattered all the way to its sandy bed.

Indosso e calzo ogni mattina forzando, come avessi sempre un altro numero, un'altra taglia. Cresco ancora nel buio, come una pianta che beve dal nero della terra. Per vestirsi bisogna perdere i rami allungati nel sonno, le foglie più tenere aperte. Puoi sentirle cadere a un tratto come per un inverno improvviso. Nello stesso istante perdi anche la coda e le ali che avevi. Da qualche parte del corpo lo senti. Non sanguini, è una privazione a cui ti hanno abituato. Non resta che cercare il tuo abito. Scivolare come un raggio, fino al calare della luce.

As if I always had another number, another size, every morning I force myself to put on clothes, shoes. I still grow in the darkness, like a plant drinking from black soil. Getting dressed demands losing the branches extending into sleep, their most tender leaves open. You can suddenly feel them falling like an unexpected winter. At the same time you also lose the tail and the wings you had. You feel it happening somewhere in your body. You're not bleeding, this is a deprivation to which they have accustomed you. Now you only need to look for your clothes. To glide like a sunray, until the light dims.

Qui ciò che cade indurisce nello spazio assegnato dal caso o dal destino. Cadendo si abbandona, perde ogni appartenenza. Inizia a crescere radici, sottili come capelli. Ma oggi il tempo è entrato, risuonando sui vetri. Le pareti si sono fatte sottili, come di membrana. Ogni stanza entrava nell'altra, sovrapposta in un gioco di dimensioni perfette. Ne restava una sola, profonda di tutte le altre. Vi entrava anche il giardino, con gli alberi, la strada di auto lente. Ti stava facendo questo, pazientemente, la pioggia. Sciogliendo una sillaba fino all'inizio dell'articolazione di un suono. Portandoti appena dopo il silenzio. In quella durata potevano fare ritorno, trovare luogo le cose.

Whatever falls here, hardens in the space assigned by chance or destiny. By falling it abandons itself, loses everything to which it belonged. Begins to grow roots, thin as hair. But today, time has entered, resounding on the windowpanes. The walls have become thin like membranes. Each room entered the next one, superimposed in a game of perfect dimensions. Only one room remained, deep with all the others. The garden also entered, with its trees, the street of slow cars. Patiently doing this to you was the rain. Unfastening a syllable right at the beginning of the articulated sound. Bearing you along just after the silence. In that lapse of time the things could return, each find their place.

Le frasi non compiute restano ruderi. C'è un intero paese in pericolo di crollo che stai sostenendo in te. Sai il dolore di ogni tegola, di ogni mattone. Un tonfo sordo nella radura del petto. Ci vorrebbe l'amore costante di qualcuno, un lavorare quieto che risuona nelle profondità del bosco. Tu che disfi la valigia, ti scordi di partire.

Unfinished sentences remain ruins. You're supporting inside yourself an entire village in danger of collapsing. You know the pain of every tile, every brick. A dull thud in the clearing of your chest. Perhaps it's someone's constant love, a calm chore resounding in the depths of the woods. You who are unpacking your suitcase, you forget to leave.

La mattina alzandoci reggiamo una brocca sulla nuca. Oltre la casa ogni strada è insicura, si apre una piccola radura di foglie. Anche quando arriviamo alla sorgente, il ritorno è difficile tra gli incroci e i rovi. Ma ciò che conta è che la brocca posi di nuovo sulla nuca la mattina dopo. Per questo con gli occhi fissiamo l'orizzonte, teniamo la nostra postura.

Getting up in the morning, we put a jug on our napes. Past the house every street is unsafe, then a small leafy clearing opens out. Even after reaching the water source, the way back is difficult because of the brambles and intersections. But what matters is that once again you place the jug on your nape the next morning. This is why we stare at the horizon, and keep our backs straight.

Ci sorvegliano dalle soglie, un occhio socchiuso. Sanno che torniamo all'ora dei pasti. Conoscono i nostri bisogni, le nostre debolezze diventate abitudini. Del nostro linguaggio comprendono il suono e l'intonazione di fondo. Portiamo loro la ciotola, e una carezza ci illude: averli avuti vicini.

With half-open eyes, they watch us from the thresholds. They know we come back at mealtimes. They know our needs, our weaknesses that have become habits. They comprehend the sounds, the basic intonations of our language. We bring them their bowls and a caress deceives us: having had them so close.

L'anziana che abita nel palazzo vicino esce ogni tanto in balcone. Spazza, stende i panni sul filo, li raccoglie, annaffia due vasi. Quando partirà, lascerà uno spazio pulito, che ha preso la forma della sua vita. Quella precisione istintiva mi guida per brevi sequenze: sposto la polvere, cambio posto alle cose. E come riemergendo da una nebbia, si spalanca un altro spazio nella mente.

The old woman who lives in the next building sometimes goes out onto her balcony. She sweeps, hangs out the washing on the line, brings the laundry back in, waters two flowerpots. When she passes on, she will leave a clean space shaped by her life. Such instinctive precision guides me for short sequences: I shift the dust, change the places of things. And as if reemerging from fog, another space gapes open in my mind.

In giardino le auto dei grandi restano aperte, a volte con la chiave inserita nel cruscotto. Puoi entrare e sederti nel posto di guida, portare tuo fratello nel sedile di fianco, gli amici dietro, oppure partire da solo, girando il volante alle curve, un po' a destra e un po' a sinistra, premendo il pedale del freno o dell'acceleratore, guardando dallo specchietto quello che resta alle spalle.

Di fronte, una stessa immagine ferma: le foglie del tiglio che si aprono nella luce, i piccoli occhi rotondi dei cocoriti in gabbia.

In the garden the grown-ups leave their cars unlocked, sometimes with the key in the ignition. You can hop into the driver's seat, place your little brother on the seat next to yours, with friends in the back, or take a ride on your own, turning the wheel at the curves, a little to the right, a little to the left, stepping on the brake or the accelerator, glancing at the rearview mirror at what's behind you.

Facing you, the same steady image: the lime tree leaves unfolding in the light, the small round eyes of the parakeets in a cage.

Oltre i gesti che tagliano, dosano, portano a cottura. Torno sempre all'inizio, alle cose com'erano: composte di se stesse, rivolte alla propria buccia. Così le addento, le macino fino alla poltiglia.

*

Più che portare alla bocca, la apro. Sospese dalla terra, cadono cose in bilico nella maturazione. Risplendono nel corpo come stelle morenti. I raggi vibrano, trovano la via degli occhi.

*

Semi di zucca sbucciati, e quelli minuscoli di sesamo, di lino: un furto che è giusto compiere. Da ogni giuntura, anche tu puoi levare il tuo volo.

*

Cospargiti un po' di farina sul palmo delle mani, gli zigomi, la fronte. Così iniziano le guerre e i passaggi di stato.
Prendi una padella, rigala d'olio.
Allineato ai punti cardinali, in possesso di tutte le tue forze, concèntrati: rompi un uovo.

Besides the gestures of slicing, dosing, cooking. I always return to the beginning, to things as they were: made up of themselves, turned back into their peels. So I bite into them, chew them to a pulp.

*

More than bringing things to my mouth, I open it. Dangling above the earth, precariously poised things drop when they're ripe. In the body, they shine like dying stars. The rays vibrate, finding their way to the eyes.

*

Shelled pumpkin seeds, tiny sesame seeds, linseed: a theft it is all right to commit. From every joint, even you can take flight.

*

Sprinkle a little flour on your palms, cheekbones, forehead. This is how wars and transformations begin.
Take a pan, oil it.
Lined up to the cardinal points, in possession of all your strength, concentrate: break an egg.

In questo paesaggio posso chiudere gli occhi e dormire, senza il rimorso di avere interrotto il narrare del treno: come si vive, come sono disposti gli alberi e le case, che cosa stanno facendo gli uomini.

Il racconto continua silenzioso, mentre penso e inseguo altre voci. È un tragitto compiuto tante volte, che basta poco a riconoscerlo. Guardo soltanto i fiumi. Il rumore delle rotaie sul ponte mi sveglia.

In this landscape I can close my eyes and sleep, without feeling remorse about interrupting the train's storytelling: how one lives, how the trees and houses are arranged, what human beings are doing.

The story continues in silence while I think, pursuing other voices. It's a journey taken so many times that little is needed to identify it. I look only at the rivers. The noise of the rails on the bridge awakens me.

Con il tuo bene continui a tessere questo spazio, a portare dettagli e densità. Il tuo bene è un filo che si rigenera di continuo formando una ragnatela. Io sono avvolta lì, un po' viva e un po' morta. Ma se svolgessi il filo e tornassi a vedere, troveresti una croce sormontata da un cerchio. Così sottile e lieve, tracciata sulla polvere. Basterebbe un tuo soffio per liberarmi.

With your goodness, you continue to weave this space, to bring details and density to it. Your goodness is a thread that regenerates itself continually, forming a spider web. I'm wrapped up in it, a bit alive, a bit dead. But if you unwound the thread and came back to see, you'd find a cross surmounted by a circle. So thin and light, drawn in the dust. A single breath from you would be enough to free me.

Ma tu porti argilla. Aggiungi altra argilla dell'inizio del mondo. Vai verso i luoghi rotti e vuoti. Sei chiamato dagli spazi caldi, un manovale sudato che sorride del suo lavoro che crolla.

Sorridi, ricomincia il tempo. Una tunica tiepida ti avvolge fino alle tempie, ti riporta in cucina, nella tinozza sul tavolo. Ti bagna i capelli, tra le mani grandi di tua madre.

But you bring clay. You add more clay from the beginning of the world. You go to the broken, empty places. You are beckoned by the warm places, a sweaty manual worker who smiles when what he has built up collapses.

You smile, time begins all over again. A warm towel envelops you up to your forehead, brings you back to the kitchen, into the tub on the table. Your mother's big hands wash your hair.

Mi porti in salvo come sollevando la parte più fragile di te. Resisti nel tumulto. Ed eccoti al varco, attraversato da scariche di luce chiara. Non hai più viso, sei fuori da ogni contorno. Soltanto luce chiara. Vorrei raccoglierti con le mani, contenerti mentre nasci, ma ti sprigioni: sei la corrente prima che non si può toccare.

You bear me to safety by raising the most fragile part of yourself. You resist amidst the tumult. And here you are at the threshold, clear light flashing through you. You no longer have a face, you're beyond all contours. Only clear light. I'd like to gather you up in my hands, take you in you while you are born, but you gush forth: you are the primal current that cannot be touched.

Eri scomparso sotto il lenzuolo. Muovevi le montagne. Franava la neve. Poi tutto era fermo. Prendevo un treno e tu silenzioso mi accompagnavi al fianco. Voltando la testa, oltre la linea di case, ti ritrovavo. «Credi che un nome possa avere luogo?»

You had vanished under the sheet, were making the mountains move. The snow was giving way. Then everything was still. I was riding on a train and you were sitting silently next to me. Whenever I turned my head, I would spot you again beyond the row of houses. "Do you think a name can take place?"

Nel tuo petto c'è una piccola faglia. Quando lo stringo o vi poso la testa c'è questo soffio d'aria. Ha l'umidità dei boschi e l'odore della terra. Le montagne vicine con i loro torrenti gelati. Da quando l'ho sentito non posso fare a meno di riconoscerlo. Anche quando, uno dopo l'altro, nella tua voce passano uccelli d'alta quota, segnando una rotta nel cielo limpido.

La faglia è in te, si allarga. Un soffio di freddo ti attraversa le costole e ti sta scomponendo. Non hai più un orecchio. Il tuo collo è svanito. Tra una spalla e l'altra si apre un buio popolato di fremiti, di richiami da ramo a ramo, su un pendio scosceso a dirotto, non attraversato da passi umani.

There is a small fault line in your chest. When I hug your chest or place my head on it there is this puff of air. It has a woodsy moistness and an earthy smell to it. The nearby mountains with their frozen torrents. Ever since I have heard it, I cannot help but recognize it. Even when high-soaring birds fly one after the other through your voice, marking out a route in the clear sky.

The fault line is inside you, it is widening. A chilly gust of wind blows through your ribs and is decomposing you. You no longer have an ear. Your neck has vanished. Between one shoulder and the other one opens a darkness peopled with shivers, with voices calling out from branch to branch, on a sheer slope uncrossed by human steps.

Nella notte ti veniva vicino un animale segnato dal suo peso. Alzava verso di te il suo umido muso senza altra forma che quella delle cose che sfiorava. Aveva un capo di sorgente che ti lambiva appena, cercandoti le labbra. Ciecamente, a tentoni, ti avrebbe travolto nella sua piena, portandoti con sé. La mattina qualcosa nel tuo corpo si muoveva: un'acqua attraversata dalla sua corrente.

At night an animal marked by its weight was coming close to you. It kept raising up to you its moist snout shaped like the things it had been brushing up against. It had a fountainhead that kept licking you, searching for your lips. Groping blindly, it would have swept you away in its flood, carrying you off with it. In the morning something inside your body was moving: a water crossed by its current.

I tuoi occhi potrebbero essere azzurri o neri. Il tuo nome potrebbe averlo chiunque. Mi è uscito dalle labbra una volta. Sono cose che capitano, e poi devo averti confuso. Ti ho stretto, sfaldavi come creta al sole. Ora riposa nella pace di chi è stato dimenticato.

Your eyes could be blue or black. Anyone could have your name. It once sprung from my lips. These things happen, and then I must have mistaken you. I hugged you tight: you crumbled like clay in the sun. Now rest in peace, of one who has been forgotten.

Piove dalle travi del tetto. Tutta la notte spilli sottili fino al sangue. Le cose mi chiamano – vestirsi, annodarsi le scarpe.

Liberata dal corpo, accarezzata dal buio. Come si cammina lo sai. Per farlo ancora, dimentica, torna a pesare sui piedi.

It's raining through the roof beams. All night long, thin needles until they reach the blood. Things call out to me— get dressed, tie your shoes.

Freed from the body, caressed by the darkness. You know how to walk. To do so again, forget, go back to weighing down on your feet.

Ti chini verso una pozza di fango. Porti le mani sul viso e lo fai scuro. Resta l'incavo degli occhi. Dalla punta delle dita alle spalle ti accarezza la terra. Il bianco dei denti chiama le ossa sommerse. Un grande animale marino dorme sotto la sabbia. Il rito è quasi concluso.

You bend over a mud puddle. Cover your face with your hands and make it dark. The eye sockets remain. From your fingertips to your shoulders, the earth caresses you. The bright white teeth call out to the submerged bones. A big sea animal sleeps beneath the sand. The ritual is almost concluded.

Sei stanca. Stai facendo spuntare le gemme. Le scorze si frangono, non resistono più. Con gli occhi chiusi continui a lottare. La terra è una roccia, si sbriciola in ghiaia sottile. È una parete e una porta. Continua a dormire. Le foglie si parlano fraterne. Dal cuore alla cima della chioma, stanno iniziando una frase per te.

You're tired. You're making the buds break out. The bark is splitting apart, no longer resisting. With closed eyes, you keep fighting. The earth is a rock, crumbling into tiny pieces of gravel. It is a wall and a door. Keep sleeping. The leaves are speaking to each other like brothers. From the heart to the crown of the tree, the leaves are thinking up a sentence for you.

Franca Mancinelli was born in Fano, Italy, in 1981. Her first book of poetry, *Mala kruna* (Manni, 2007), won the L'Aquila First Book Award as well as the Giuseppe Giusti Prize. Her second book, *Pasta madre* (with a postface by Milo De Angelis; Nino Aragno Editore, 2013), was then awarded the Alpi Apuane, the Carducci, and the Ceppo-Giovani Prizes. A selection of poems from the latter volume initially appeared in *Nuovi poeti italiani 6*, edited by Giovanna Rosadini (Einaudi, 2012). Her work has also been featured in several anthologies, including *XIII Quaderno italiano di poesia contemporanea* (Marcos y Marcos, 2017), edited by Franco Buffoni. As a critic, she contributes to *Poesia* and other literary journals. She is an editor for the literary review *Smerilliana*, the poetry magazine *Argo–annuario di poesia*, and the blog *Interno poesia*. Her writing has been translated into Spanish, Arabic, and Slovene, and her first two books have been recently reprinted as *A un'ora di sonno da qui* (At an hour's sleep from here) by Italic & Pequod. In 2018 appeared the original Italian edition of this collection of prose poems, *Libretto di transito* (Amos Edizioni). *The Little Book of Passage* marks the first appearance of her work in English.

John Taylor is an American writer, critic, and translator who is originally from Des Moines and has long lived in France. His translations of Italian and French poetry have been awarded grants and prizes from the National Endowment for the Arts, the Academy of American Poets, and the Sonia Raiziss Charitable Foundation. His translation of José-Flore Tappy's poetry (*Sheds*, Bitter Oleander Press, 2014) was a finalist for the National Translation Award in 2015. For the Bitter Oleander Press, he has also translated books by Jacques Dupin and Pierre Voélin. Among the many other writers and poets whom he has translated are Phillippe Jaccottet, Pierre-Albert Jourdan, Georges Perros, Catherine Colomb, Pierre Chappuis, Lorenzo Calogero, and Alfredo de Palchi. He is the author of several volumes of short prose and poetry, most recently *If Night is Falling* (Bitter Oleander Press), *The Dark Brightness* (Xenos Books), *Grassy Stairways* (The MadHat Press), and *Remembrance of Water & Twenty-Five Trees* (Bitter Oleander Press).

THE BITTER OLEANDER PRESS
Library of Poetry

—TRANSLATION SERIES—

Torn Apart by Joyce Mansour $14.00
(France)   *—translated by Serge Gavronsky*

Children of the Quadrilateral by Benjamin Péret
(France)   *—translated by Jane Barnard & Albert Frank Moritz* $14.00

Edible Amazonia by Nicomedes Suárez-Araúz $11.00
(Bolivia)   *—translated by Steven Ford Brown*

A Cage of Transparent Words by Alberto Blanco
(Mexico)   *—a bilingual edition with multiple translators* $20.00

Afterglow by Alberto Blanco $21.00
(Mexico)   *—translated by Jennifer Rathbun*

Of Flies and Monkeys by Jacques Dupin $24.00
(France)   *—translated by John Taylor*

1001 Winters by Kristiina Ehin $21.00
(Estonia)   *—translated by Ilmar Lehtpere*

Tobacco Dogs by Ana Minga $18.00
(Ecuador)   *—translated by Alexis Levitin*

Sheds by José-Flore Tappy * $21.00
(Switzerland) *—translated by John Taylor*

Puppets in the Wind by Karl Krolow $21.00
(Germany)   *—translated by Stuart Friebert*

Movement Through the End by Philippe Rahmy $18.00
(Switzerland) *—translated by Rosemary Lloyd*

Ripened Wheat: Selected Poems of Hai Zi ** $21.00
(China)   *—translated by Ye Chun*

Conmfetti-Ash: Selected Poems of Salvador Novo $18.00
(Mexico)   *—translated by Anthony Seidman & David Shook*

* Finalist for National Translation Award from American Literary Translators Association (ALTA)—2015

** Finalist for Lucien Stryk Asian Translation Award from American Literary Translators Association (ALTA)—2016

*** Long-Listed for National Translation Award from American Literary Translators Association (ALTA)—2017

THE BITTER OLEANDER PRESS
Library of Poetry

—ORIGINAL POETRY SERIES—

The Moon Rises in the Rattlesnake's Mouth by Silvia Scheibli	$ 6.00
On Carbon-Dating Hunger by Anthony Seidman	$14.00
Where Thirsts Intersect by Anthony Seidman	$16.00
Festival of Stone by Steve Barfield	$12.00
Infinite Days by Alan Britt	$16.00
Vermilion by Alan Britt	$16.00
Teaching Bones to Fly by Christine Boyka Kluge	$14.00
Stirring the Mirror by Christine Boyka Kluge	$16.00
Travel Over Water by Ye Chun	$14.00
Gold Carp Jack Fruit Mirrors by George Kalamaras	$18.00
Van Gogh in Poems by Carol Dine	$21.00
** *Giving Way* by Shawn Fawson	$16.00
If Night is Falling by John Taylor	$16.00
The First Decade: 1968-1978 by Duane Locke	$25.00
Empire in the Shade of a Grass Blade by Rob Cook	$18.00
**Painting the Egret's Echo* by Patty Dickson Pieczka [2012]	$14.00
Parabola Dreams by Alan Britt & Silvia Scheibli	$16.00
Child Sings in the Womb by Patrick Lawler	$18.00
* *The Cave* by Tom Holmes [2013]	$12.00
Light from a Small Brown Bird by Rich Ives	$14.00

* Winner of The Bitter Oleander Press Library of Poetry Award (BOPLOPA)
** Utah Book Award Winner (2012)
*** Typography, Graphic Design & Poetry

All back issues and single copies of *The Bitter Oleander* are available for $10.00
For more information, contact us at info@bitteroleander.com
Visit us on Facebook or www.bitteroleander.com